D0604831

DATE DUE			
DEC 1 1 1996			

THE LIBRARY STORE   #47-0120

A World of Difference

On Your Feet!

By Karin Luisa Badt

Consultant
Jonathan Walford, Curator, The Bata Shoe Museum, Toronto, Canada

CHILDRENS PRESS®
CHICAGO

Picture Acknowledgments

Cover (top left), NASA; Cover (3 photos), 1, Bata Shoe Museum; 3 (top right), © Porterfield/Chickering; 3 (bottom right), The Bettmann Archive; 3 (bottom left), Bata Shoe Museum; 4 (left), North Wind Picture Archives; 4 (right), 5 (top), Archive Photos; 5 (bottom), © Reinhard Brucker, Anasazi Heritage Center, Delores, Colorado; 6 (bottom left), © Ray Webber/Bata Shoe Museum; 6 (top right), Bata Shoe Museum, 6 (bottom right), Photri; 7 (top), © W. Luthy/Photri; 7 (bottom right), 8 (left & top right), Bata Shoe Museum; 8 (bottom right), H. Armstrong Roberts; 9 (left), UPI/Bettmann; 9 (right), © Tony Boxall/Photri; 10 (left), The Bettmann Archive; 10 (right), © AKG/SuperStock; 11 (top & bottom right), Bata Shoe Museum; 11 (bottom left), © Phil Norton/Valan; 12 (top), Bata Shoe Museum; 12 (bottom), © Nancy Simmerman/Tony Stone Images; 13 (left), H. Armstrong Roberts; 13 (top right), © Arthur Strange/Valan; 13 (center right), Bata Shoe Museum; 13 (bottom right), © Ray Webber/Bata Shoe Museum; 14 (top), © Kennon Cooke/Valan; 14 (bottom), Photri; 15 (top), © Virginia R. Grimes; 15 (bottom), © Camerique; 16 (left & top right), Bata Shoe Museum; 16-17 (bottom), The Bettmann Archive; 17 (top left), Gift of Lauren Bacall, © Irving Solero/Courtesy of the Museum at Fashion Institute of Technology; 17 (right), North Wind Picture Archives; 18 (left), The Bettmann Archive; 18 (top right & center right), 19 (bottom), Bata Shoe Museum; 19 (top), H. Armstrong Roberts; 20 (left), © Peter Sickles/SuperStock; 20 (top right), © Camerique; 20 (bottom right), © Kennon Cooke/Valan; 21 (top), © Virginia R. Grimes; 21 (bottom), © Michael Rutherford/SuperStock; 22 (left), Bata Shoe Museum; 22 (top right), © Ken Patterson/Valan; 22 (bottom right), © Diana Rasche/Tony Stone Images; 23 (bottom), © Michel Bourque/Valan; 23 (top), Bata Shoe Museum; 24 (left), © Tony Freeman/PhotoEdit; 24(top right), © John Eastcott/Yva Momatiuk/Valan; 24 (bottom right), Tony Stone Images; 25 (left), © B. Templeman /Valan; 25 (top right), © Dennis O'Clair/Tony Stone Images; 25 (center right) © Fred Bruemmer/Valan; 25 (bottom right), © Virginia R. Grimes; 26 (left), © John Elk III; 26 (top right and center right), Bata Shoe Museum; 26 (bottom right), © Reinhard Brucker; 27 (top left), © Cameramann International, Ltd.; 27 (bottom right), Photri; 27 (right), © Jane P. Downton/Root Resources; 28 (left), © Rich Henry/Photri; 28 (top), Bata Shoe Museum; 28 (bottom right), © Porterfield/Chickering; 29 (top), © A.B. Joyce/Valan; 29 (center), © Nicole Katano/Tony Stone Images; 29 (bottom) Designer Jean-Paul Gaultier 1986, © Irving Solero/Courtesy of The Museum at Fashion Institute of Technology; 30 (bottom), North Wind Picture Archives; 30 (top), © Cameramann International, Ltd.; 31 (top left), © John Eastcott/Yva Momatiuk/Valan; 31 (top right), © Virginia R. Grimes; 31 (center), © Lucy Horne/Photri; 31 (bottom right), © Cameramann International, Ltd.

The author and editor wish to thank the Bata Shoe Museum Foundation for its kind support, and for providing invaluable information during the development of this project.

On the cover

Top: Hausa sandal, northern Nigeria
or southern Niger
Middle: English brocade shoe, 1730s
Bottom: *Ghatela* from Lucknow, India,
late 1800s

On the title page

Royal toe-knob sandals, Zaire, 1800s

Project Editor Shari Joffe
Design Beth Herman Design Associates
Photo Research Feldman & Associates

Badt, Karin Luisa.
    On Your Feet! / by Karin Luisa Badt.
        p. cm. — (A World of Difference)
    Includes index.
    ISBN 0-516-08189-6
    1. Shoes–Juvenile Literature. [1. Shoes.] I. Title
II. Series.
GT2130.B24   1994
391` .413`09 —dc20   94-11651
                                                         CIP
                                                         AC

Copyright 1994 by Childrens Press®, Inc.
All rights reserved. Published simultaneously in Canada.
Printed in the United States of America.
` 2 3 4 5 6 7 8 9 10 R 03 02 01 00 99 98 97 96 95

Contents

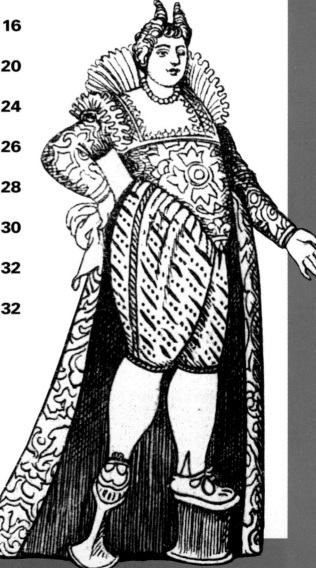

Watch Your Step!

"Give me a pair of boots, Sir," said the smart cat
to his poor master, *"and I will make you a rich
and happy man!"*
—"Puss In Boots"

*"There's no place like home! There's no place
like home!"* said Dorothy, clicking her ruby shoes.
*Suddenly she was no longer in Oz, but back
in Kansas, with her Aunty Em.*
—The Wizard of Oz

*Cinderella slipped her foot into the glass slipper.
If it fit, she would become a princess!*
—"Cinderella"

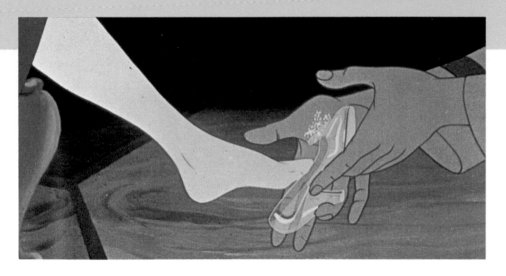

Cinderella's glass slipper
Special or magical shoes have appeared in many folktales and fairy tales.

Anasazi straw sandal
The Anasazi people lived in parts of present-day Arizona, Colorado, and New Mexico from about A.D. 100 to 1400. Like the earliest shoes, theirs were made mainly to protect the feet, and were very simple in design.

How amazing shoes are in fairy tales! Put them on, and WOW! All sorts of wonderful things are possible.

But is it really any different in real life? *Your* shoes are amazing too! If you didn't have a pair, could you play in the snow or run in the woods? Could you walk on a hot sidewalk or kick a ball? You would always be afraid of stepping on something too hot or too cold, too wet or too prickly . . . OUCH!

Without shoes, people in certain parts of the world would find it hard to leave their homes. Imagine trying to cross a hot desert or a rocky mountain barefoot! That would be quite a feat, don't you think?

People who lived back in the Stone Age, about 25,000 years ago, probably thought so too. But what could they do? Shoes weren't invented yet! So they took animal skins and wrapped them around their feet.

Later, people became more fussy about their footwear. It occurred to them that not only do shoes keep your feet warm and safe, but they can make your feet look special.

Straw, Wood, or Leather?

If you were going to make a shoe, what would you use? Gold and emeralds? Pizza crust? How about a piece of paper?

Today, you could go to the store and choose from many different materials to make your shoes. But that has not always been the case. Until a few hundred years ago, transportation was very difficult. People could not trade as easily as they can today. They had to make their shoes out of the materials they could find in their own environment.

For example, the Inuit by the Arctic Ocean made boots out of sealskin, Scandinavians made shoes out of tree bark, and the Japanese made sandals out of rice straw.

Hindu kharrow
This foot-shaped sandal, worn in India in the 1700s or 1800s, is made out of zinc!

Peruvian tire sandals
In some places, people have made shoes from recycled materials. These sandals are made of old tires. They are durable, yet cool enough for the hot climate of Peru.

Japanese *waraji* These sandals are made from rice straw, a material plentiful in Japan.

Inuit sealskin boots, Greenland The Inuit live along the Arctic Ocean, where sea mammals are plentiful. They make their warm, protective boots from sealskin.

Bark *lapti,* Finland or Siberia These shoes have been woven out of a material found in many parts of the world—tree bark!

7

In the past, people could tell something about the environment you lived in by looking at your shoes. Your shoes told clues about what kinds of materials were available in your land, and what the climate was like. If your shoes were made of wood, you were probably from a land covered with dark forests. If they were made of fur, your land was cold and full of wild animals. Straw shoes? Why, that would mean you're from a sunny place where grass grows plentifully!

Peruvian sisal sandal
These sandals are made of sisal, a strong fiber that comes from a plant native to Central and South America.

East African leather sandal
These leather sandals are tough, yet lightweight. This makes them perfect for the rough desert regions of eastern Africa.

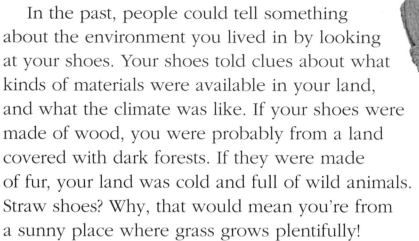

Sheepherder, Dolomite Alps, Italy Leather, available in many countries throughout the world, is one of the most common materials used to make shoes.

Clogs Wooden clogs have been popular in many places where there are trees. Men and women wear clogs in Pakistan, England, Germany, Brazil, France, the Middle East, central Africa, and the United States. They are very inexpensive and easy to make. Fishermen like them because they can wade in the water with them.

Clogs During World War II, when leather was scarce, many people wore clogs.

LA JOLLA COUNTRY DAY SCHOOL
LIBRARY
9490 Genesee Ave.
La Jolla, CA 92037

Don't Go Out Without Your Boots!

The sandal was the first shoe invented after the Stone Age, during the early days of recorded history. That is because civilization began in the warm part of the globe. The sandal kept the foot cool under a hot sun. People's shoes fit the weather! Ancient Egyptians wore sandals made of palm leaves and papyrus. The sandals were tied to their feet with straps.

Ancient Greeks and Romans also lived in a warm climate. They wore sandals that looked a lot like the early Egyptian sandal. They were made of leather, and tied up the leg.

Ancient Egyptian sandal

Ancient Roman sandal

Swedish Sami boot The Sami people live in a region called Lapland, which lies above the Arctic Circle in the northern parts of Norway, Sweden, Finland, and Russia. Many Sami are nomadic and keep herds of reindeer. Winter lasts nine months in Lapland, so warm winter boots made of reindeer fur are a necessity!

Even today, people often wear the traditional shoes of their country. On some mornings in Russia, children are told to put on their *valenki* because it is snowing outside. A *valenki* is a boot made completely of felt. Have you ever touched felt? It is soft and warm. Even the soles of the *valenki* are made of felt.

Russian *valenki*

Snowshoes, Quebec, Canada Snowshoes help people walk through deep, soft snow without sinking.

Up high in the Himalaya Mountains, Tibetans keep warm with boots made from the hide of the hairy yak. Yaks are big, shaggy animals that live only in central Asia, where Tibet is located.

In the Philippines, you would never find a shoe made of yak fur. There, a popular shoe is the *sapato,* which is made of coconut shells. The climate in the Philippines is hot and wet, and coconuts grow easily there. In Mexico, which is hot and dry, the Nahua people, a Native American group, keep cool with sandals made of yucca leaves.

Hawaiian ti-leaf sandal Don't these sandals look cool? They're made from the leaves and branches of the ti plant, which grows in Asia and on many Pacific islands.

Tibetan boots
The soles of these colorful boots from Tibet are made of yak hide; the uppers are made of wool.

The Japanese have a traditional shoe called the *yuki geta*. It has two "stilts" on the bottom, which makes it useful for walking in wet, muddy, or snowy areas.

In Ireland, some people wear shoes called *brogues,* which completely cover the foot. *Brogues* have holes in them so that water can drain out after a person walks across a marshy bog.

Shoes from two distant cultures can sometimes look very much alike—even though the two cultures may never have had any contact with each other! How is this so? Because people who live far apart, but in the same *kind* of climate, tend to invent the same kind of shoes. For example, the *yuki geta* looks a lot like the Spanish wooden shoe shown below. Both are a piece of wood with stilts on the bottom—and both were designed to lift one's feet above wetness and dirt.

Japanese yuki geta

Masai woman, Kenya In some countries where the climate is very hot, some of the people wear no shoes at all. The bottoms of their feet become hard with callouses. This protects their feet very much like the sole of a shoe would.

Dutch patten, 1400s During the Middle Ages, Europeans strapped overshoes, called pattens, onto their regular shoes to keep them out of the mud of the streets.

Spanish wooden shoe The Japanese *yuki geta*, the Dutch patten, and this Spanish wooden shoe all look similar—because all three were designed to lift one's feet above wetness and dirt.

Shoes Give Clues to a Culture's Views

What's so interesting about other people's shoes? Everything! The style of a shoe can reflect the values of a culture: what people believe in and how they approach life. For example, the Amish, members of a devout Protestant sect, believe in living life as simply as possible. They live in self-contained communities in Pennsylvania, Ohio, Indiana, Illinois, and Iowa, and do not use any modern technology, such as cars, telephones, or electricity. So it's not surprising that their clothes and shoes are also very simple. Their plain style of dress also reflects their wish to avoid anything that might indicate worldly vanity.

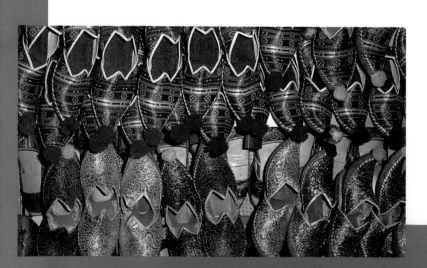

Mennonite shoes Mennonites, like the Amish, believe in living a simple life. This is reflected in their shoes and clothes, which are very plain and have no decoration. Mennonites have worn this same style of dress for centuries.

Turkish slippers Traditionally, shoes and clothing made of beautiful, rich-looking fabrics have been highly valued in Turkish culture.

American sneaker In the United States today, many people wear sneakers, even when they are not playing sports. Businesswomen, for example, may wear sneakers to get to work, and then change into more elegant shoes at the office. Sneakers are very comfortable, practical shoes. They are easily adaptable to the variety of settings that many Americans walk through in a single day.

Where You Stand

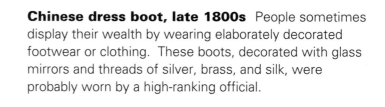

Shoes can say something about a person's place in society—in other words, their social status. Sometimes, people wear a certain style of shoe to show how rich and powerful they are. In ancient Rome, only senators were allowed to wear black sandals. Roman peasants wore short boots called *peros.* In twelfth-century Germany, princes fought with the Pope for the right to wear the *sandalia,* a special boot decorated with pearls. Whoever wore this special boot was considered to be very powerful.

"Cow-mouth" shoe, 1500s The *Kuhmaulschuh,* which has a toe shaped like the mouth of a cow, was popular among wealthy Europeans in the 1500s. German painter Albrecht Dürer (1471-1528) liked to wear these shoes to show that he was an important person.

Chinese dress boot, late 1800s People sometimes display their wealth by wearing elaborately decorated footwear or clothing. These boots, decorated with glass mirrors and threads of silver, brass, and silk, were probably worn by a high-ranking official.

Middle Eastern slipper In ancient Sumer, shoes with turned-up points were considered so special that only kings and princes were allowed to wear them. Today, pointy shoes are still worn in many Middle Eastern countries—but no longer only by the privileged.

Crackowe, 1400s In Europe in the Middle Ages, everyone wanted to wear long, pointy shoes, called crackowes. They were named after the city of Krakow, Poland, where they first became popular. Both men and women wore them. The pointier your shoe was, the more important you were. Sometimes the toe was so long that if you were sitting at a dinner table, the point reached the other side! In England, princes and dukes were permitted to wear crackowes that were as much as thirty inches long, while commoners were allowed only six inches. The Pope tried to make crackowes illegal in 1468. He said they were "a worldly vanity and a mad presumption."

French illustration, 1400s This illustration from a French book of the 1400s shows people wearing crackowes, which were so popular at the time.

The richer you are, the more comfortable your shoes . . . right? WRONG! In some cultures, wealthy people have worn shoes that are impossible to walk in, just to show how well-off they are! Only rich people can afford not to walk. They can pay other people to do physical work for them. In sixteenth-century Europe, it was the fashion for wealthy people to wear chopines. Chopines were sometimes nearly three feet tall! Women who wore them could barely walk, and had to be supported by their servants.

Paduka, southern India, 1700s These special sandals were probably worn by a Hindu priest or some other member of upper-class Indian society. They are made of silver pressed over wood and have toeknobs made of gold!

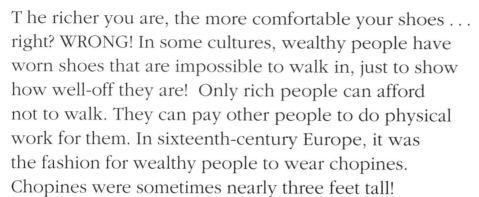

Chopine, 1500s

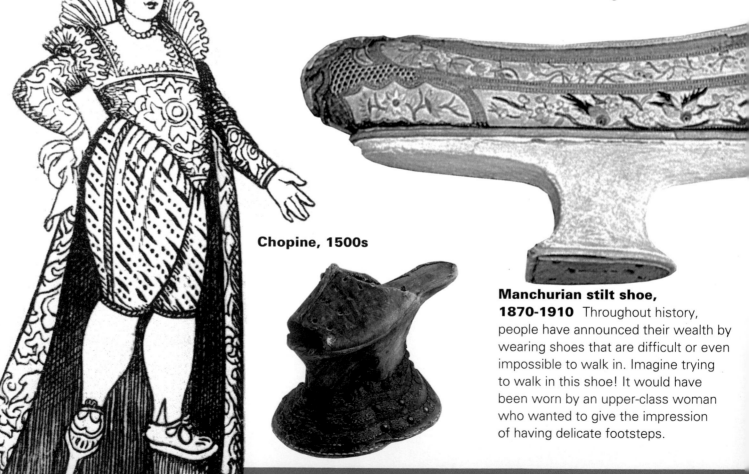

Manchurian stilt shoe, 1870-1910 Throughout history, people have announced their wealth by wearing shoes that are difficult or even impossible to walk in. Imagine trying to walk in this shoe! It would have been worn by an upper-class woman who wanted to give the impression of having delicate footsteps.

King Louis XIV (1638-1715)

Up until recently, both men and women wore high heels when they wanted to look important. French king Louis XIV wore heels that were four inches high! This was one way he could show that he was "higher" than everyone else. Today, a curved heel is called a "Louis heel." After the French Revolution in 1789, the French middle class stopped wearing high heels for a time. They wanted to show that their values were more down-to-earth than those of the old nobility.

English brocade shoe, 1730s

For a long time, the Louis heel was fashionable throughout Europe.

Work Shoes

Construction worker

Your shoes can say something about what you are going to do in them. For example, sometimes you need a certain type of shoe to do a certain type of work. Construction workers wear thick, sturdy, protective boots because their work can be dirty, physical, and dangerous. Ballet dancers, on the other hand, wear flexible, lightweight slippers because they need to be able to move around easily. It would be pretty hard to dance in a pair of boots!

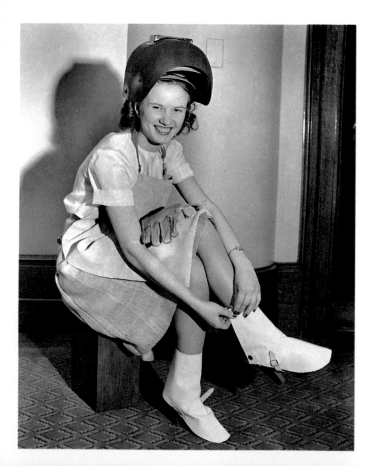

American defense worker, 1940s Protective footgear was part of the uniform worn by this 1940s defense-plant worker. The shortage of male workers during World War II gave American women the chance to prove that they could succeed at jobs previously open only to men.

Sponge diver, Florida This sponge diver from Tarpon Springs, Florida, wears special boots to help weigh him down and to protect his feet from underwater obstacles.

Professional dancers, Azerbaijan Most professional dancers do their work in flexible shoes or slippers. Some dancers wear out hundreds of pairs of shoes during their career.

American cowboy boot Boots were originally worn to protect people against snakebite and thorny plants. In the Middle Ages, people began to wear boots for horseback riding to protect their feet and legs. What do cowboys do? They ride horses! That is why they wear boots.

Military recruits, Saskatchewan, Canada

Austrian Wellington Boot, 1800s The boot is also the shoe that most soldiers wear. Boots were first mass-produced for war in the 1600s. Not only do they protect the leg well above the ankle, but they also help soldiers feel that they are part of a uniform group. George Patton, a famous American general, once said, "What is a soldier without his boots?"

Surgeon's slippers Before performing surgery, surgeons put on sterile paper slippers to prevent the spread of germs in the operating room.

Traditionally, many American Indian tribes wore a comfortable shoe called moccasins. Why? Because they are excellent footwear for hunting. They are very flexible, and since they are so soft, you can move in them without making any noise.

Sometimes a certain kind of shoe is worn as part of a uniform. This helps other people instantly identify someone as belonging to a certain profession. In the United States, nurses and other hospital workers usually wear white shoes. In Japan, until recently, you could tell a fireman by his square straw sandals (*setta*), a gardener by his wooden clogs (*niwa-geta*), and a general by his bearskin boots (*kamogutsu*). Businesspeople throughout the world generally wear shoes that are somewhat formal, to help them look professional.

Delaware/Caddo moccasins, 1800s The moccasin is the traditional shoe of many Native American groups. It is made from a single piece of soft leather that is sewn at the top. Moccasins have always been considered excellent footwear for hunting, because a person can move in them so easily and quietly.

Schoolgirls, Ecuador
Adults aren't the only ones who sometimes wear shoes as part of a uniform!

Play Shoes

When work is through for the day, people put on all different kinds of shoes to help them play!

Horseback rider, Ireland

Flippers

Soccer players, United States

Rollerblader, United States

Tobogganers, Greenland

Ice climber, Canada

Ice skates, China

25

Standing on Ceremony

On special occasions, such as weddings, people often wear special shoes. Sometimes, shoes that are part of a culture's traditional dress are worn during special festivals or ceremonies.

Plains Indian dancer, Oklahoma

Ashanti crocodile sandals, Ghana Sandals like these would be worn by an Ashanti shaman, or healer, during a special ceremony.

Malaysian wedding slipper, 1950s

Iroquois corn-husk slippers
Traditionally, corn had special meaning for the Iroquois, as it was one of their most important crops. When Iroquois people died, they sometimes were buried in special funerary sandals like these.

In some countries, people wear special shoes inside their homes. This is because the home is viewed as a special place. It is considered very bad manners in these cultures to wear indoors the shoes you normally wear outdoors. In Turkey, China, Japan, and many African countries, for example, guests take off their shoes at the door and put on special slippers. In Algeria and Morocco, the slipper worn inside the house is called a *babouche*.

Muslim mosque, Jerusalem Muslims, Hindus, and Orthodox Jews all must remove their shoes before entering their places of worship. This is done as a sign of respect and to show that one is humble before one's God.

MOSQUE: PLEASE REMOVE YOUR SHOES
यह मसजिद है
कृपया जूते उतार दीजिये
مسجد ہے مہربانی کر کے جوتے اتار دیجیے

Japanese home In Japan, people park their regular shoes at the door before going inside their homes. Slippers are worn in corridors, and no shoes at all are worn inside the rooms.

Express Yourself!

As you can see, shoes say a lot! They can say something about where you are from, what you like to do, and what your social status is. They even tell us if you are going to a special occasion!

But most of all, shoes say something about your personality. You choose what to wear on your feet. Are you wearing ripped, old shoes? Well, maybe you are a person who likes to be casual. Are you wearing shoes with pink elephants on them? Maybe you are a funny person! Are you wearing the same shoes your friends are? Maybe you like to follow the fashion. Following the fashion can help people feel that they fit into their group.

Some people like to wear very fancy shoes. Julius Caesar, ruler of ancient Rome, liked to wear boots decorated with gold! Native Americans liked to decorate their footware with porcupine quills, silk ribbons, animal hair, and glass beads. There are millions of ways to decorate a shoe and make it look as special as you are!

Sioux quilled shoe, late 1800s

Children's shoes, Korea

Doc Martens This style of boot became fashionable among American and European teenagers in the 1980s.

School playground, Australia
Different people like to wear different kinds of shoes.

Sneakers, United States
Shoes can be a great way to express your personality!

In fact, a shoe can be a work of art! Like art, it expresses the soul . . . or is it, the sole?

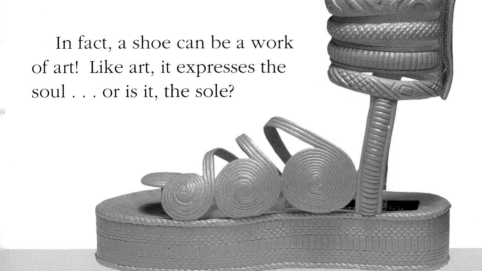

Gaultier shoe, 1980s This fun plastic shoe, created by a famous French clothing designer, was probably inspired by ancient Roman sandals.

Put Yourself in My Shoes

Some of the magic of the shoe has been lost in recent times. Today, most shoes are made in factories. And because trade is so widespread, people can—and commonly do—wear shoes that come from faraway countries. This means that, to some extent, "traditional" footwear is becoming a thing of the past. In the Middle East, for example, you will find more people wearing American sneakers than traditional pointy-toe slippers!

But the production of footwear in factories is also a good thing. When shoes could be made only by hand, not everyone who wanted a pair could have one. They cost far too much money. Today you can try on many different sizes and choose the pair that is most comfortable for you.

Shoe factory, Mexico
Today, most shoes are made in factories.

And in many cases, rather than losing traditions, people are finding and preserving them. The world has become a smaller place because of widespread trade and travel. It is easier than ever to learn about and borrow traditions from many lands. We can wear shoe styles from around the world!

Medieval shoemaker's workshop Until about 150 years ago, most shoes were made by hand. Shoes were first produced in factories in the 1860s, after the invention of the sewing machine.

What kind of shoes are you wearing? Do you know where they were invented? Perhaps you are wearing sneakers. These were invented about a hundred years ago in the United States, after the invention of processed rubber. Or perhaps you are wearing *brogues*— a kind of shoe that was originally Irish. What about in the summer? Have you ever worn flip-flops with a thong between your toes? That style comes from Ancient Egypt.

The shoe has walked a long way.

From New York to Berlin to Seoul Because cultures around the world are exchanging ideas and styles more than ever before, some kinds of shoes— like sneakers—can be found in every part of the globe!

Air Jordans In the 1980s and 1990s, kids around the world wanted to wear the same sneakers as basketball superstar Michael Jordan.

Glossary

ancient very old (p.10)

callouses hard, thickened areas of skin (p.13)

civilization a complex society with a stable food supply, division of labor, some form of government, and a highly developed culture (p.10)

climate the average weather conditions of a place or region over a period of years (p.8)

culture the beliefs and customs of a group of people that are passed from one generation to another (p.13)

durable able to last a long time (p.6)

elaborate having much detail (p.16)

environment a person's natural surroundings (p.6)

fashion the style that is popular at a particular time (p.28)

fiber a long, slender, threadlike material that can be spun into yarn (p.8)

flexible bendable; not stiff (p.23)

humble not bold or proud; modest (p.27)

inspire to be the source of or influence for (p.29)

material the substance that something is made of (p.8)

nomadic referring to people who move with their flocks or herds as the seasons change (p.11)

papyrus an African plant that grows especially in Egypt (p.10)

preserve to keep or save; to protect (p.31)

privileged having rights or liberties granted to some people but not to others (p.17)

professional acting in a businesslike manner in the workplace (p.23)

recycle to use over again (p.6)

social status the position or rank of a person within his or her society (p.16)

traditional handed down from generation to generation (p.11)

transportation the means by which people or goods are moved from one place to another (p.6)

values the ideas and ways of behaving that are viewed as important by a given people (p.14)

Index

About the Author

Karin Luisa Badt has a Ph.D. in comparative literature from the University of Chicago and a B.A. in literature and society from Brown University. She likes to travel and live in foreign countries. Ms. Badt has taught at the University of Rome and the University of Chicago.